Fabulous TeeShirt Quilts

Fabulous TeeSHIRT Quilts

by Caryl Schuetz

Southern Life Publishing Services, LLC

Montgomery, Alabama

DEDICATION
To my family and my quilting friends.

ACKNOWLEDGEMENTS

I am grateful to my grandmother, Sophie Koczera Schick, from whom I got the bug of loving fabric and wanting to play and work with it when I was but a tad. (Could it be genetic?)

Thank you to Maury, my husband, who was the one who got me involved with collecting antique quilts many years ago; and my sons, Jay and Tevlin, for their encouragement and support, especially to Tevlin for his creative artist's input. I am also indebted to Sally Schuetz, who gave me some 1930's "Dresden Plate" quilt blocks that she had found in her attic; they inspired me to learn to make quilts.

My gratitude goes to Suzy Rizzo and Cathy Franks, dear quiltmaking friends who have always been there for me. Also to Anita Harden and Jane Lee, who were in my very first tee shirt quilt workshop, and whose quilts are in this book. I thank fellow members of Art Quilters Alliance and Women of Cloth for their support, and very importantly, my students, who have taught me and kept me on my toes over the years.

Kaye England is a dear friend who has been very good to me. (I worked and taught in her quilt shops.) She introduced me to my publisher, Sunshine Huff (aka Mary Elizabeth Johnson). How lucky was that! And where would I be without Sunshine, with her expertise and her kindness! Thank you.

For information on the author, including a listing of lectures and classes she offers, contact her at:

Caryl Schuetz
Post Office Box 68827 Trader's Point
Indianapolis, Indiana 46268
Phone: 317-293-2466 Fax: 317-293-0555
Website: www.quiltvalues.com

ISBN: 0-9711168-3-0

Produced by
Southern Life Publishing Services, LLC
1283 Westmoreland Avenue
Montgomery, Alabama 36106
mejbooks@bellsouth.net

Project Editor: Mary Elizabeth Johnson
Graphic Designer: Rachel Prosser
Photography: Caryl Schuetz
Author photograph: Jay Schuetz
"Joy" and "A Writerly Quilt" photographs: Rachel Prosser
Production Manager: John Huff

Cover quilt: "Memories," made by the author in Indianapolis, 2005. 41" X 41".
Collection of the author, Indianapolis, Indiana.

Contents

"Joy," designed by Mary Elizabeth Johnson in Montgomery, Alabama, in 2004. Assembled and quilted by Angela Taylor, New Traditions Machine Quilting, Birmingham, Alabama, in 2004. 70" X 86". Collection of Mary Elizabeth Johnson and John Huff, Montgomery, Alabama.

The different tee shirt designs on this quilt come from places and times of fun, relaxation, amusement and entertainment with friends and family. The collection of motifs seemed to lend itself to purple, and a mottled print in medium tones proved to be exactly the right unifying element, especially when combined with dark borders. The quilt back is a fabulous Kaffe Fassett print featuring rhubarb.

Introduction

Make A Really Fabulous Tee Shirt Quilt

began quilting in the early seventies and started teaching twenty years later. One of my earliest classes was on how to make keepsake quilts, those lovely, unique works that document the maker's recollections of people, places, and events. As the class met week after week, I taught several different techniques, including how to transfer photos onto fabric for sewing into a quilt.

One day as we were manufacturing fabric motifs from the computer, I had a "Eureka!" moment: I realized that there was a trove of ready-made motifs available for the taking—those on tee shirts. After all, most tee shirts are specifically designed to help a person recall a special place or event. "Aha!" I thought. "We can apply the same ideas from our beautiful keepsake quilts to making fabulous tee shirt quilts." Although I am sure there must have been others doing the same thing at that time, I knew nothing about it: I was pleased to have come up with the new idea.

I scheduled my first workshop on making tee shirt quilts for sometime in early 1991. I made up a sample and hung it in the quilt shop where I worked, hoping to attract potential students. Reaction was very positive, and five quilters signed up. (I am so pleased that students from that original class have quilts in this book!)

Since then, I have taught tee shirt quilt classes more than fifty times. I am immensely gratified that my students seem to enjoy them so much. A couple of my students have even gone "pro," accepting commissions to make tee shirt quilts for other people.

This book gives you the same information I provide to my students. It explains how to turn treasured tee shirts into very personal, and very beautiful, quilts. No two are alike (unless you deliberately make them the same), and all remind their recipients of meaningful times or events. A tee shirt quilt is sort of like a scrapbook, but it's better because you can sleep under it!

The motifs printed on tee shirts are usually quite colorful and attractive. Many of them are the brain children of talented graphic designers, and they are created to stimulate the eye and the mind. A quilt made of an artful arrangement of these motifs is a visual delight and wonderful conversation piece.

Innovative display of the motifs is one of the secrets to the beauty of these quilts: the other is the incorporation of striking fabrics to provide visual boosts or unifying elements. As you examine the examples in this book, take note of the fabrics in the sashings and borders; some of them seem to call out for notice, others lend a more subtle touch.

Often a tee shirt quilt takes on a particular theme—of sports, a special vacation or travel experience, a school activity or interest, or a hobby. Tee shirts are given or bought as souvenirs for these and many other activities. Over time, storage space can become packed to the max. Making a tee shirt quilt provides a legitimate reason, plus a method, for editing and pruning an over-abundant tee shirt collection. As few as one or two, or as many as a dozen or more, tee shirt motifs—each one individual and extremely different from the others—can be blended into a cohesive and dramatic design. In every case, the result is truly a quilt that illustrates the principle of "a whole greater than the sum of its parts."

Because these quilts are so attractive and so meaningful to the people you make them for, I believe that once you learn the basic principles and techniques, you will make a fabulous tee shirt quilt whenever you have a little window of time.

"The View," made by the author in Indianapolis in 2005. Collection of the author.

I wanted a memento of a special trip to Colorado, and when I found this wonderful design on a tee shirt, I knew I had it. The motif is so beautiful that I decided to use it by itself on a wall quilt, and I set about looking for a fabric to complement it. Nothing seemed right until I hand-dyed some fabric, then realized it was perfect for this quilt. I cut the motif from the tee shirt in a free-form fashion, rather than shin a rectangle or square, and after completing the piece, I couched a fancy nubby yarn around the undulating edge.

"The Black Quilt," made by the author in Fairhaven, Massachusetts in 2004. 58" X 70". Collection of M.J. Schuetz, Jr., Indianapolis. Quilted by Cathy Franks, Carmel, Indiana.

Even though some of the tee shirts in this quilt were very loved, and had grayed from use and many launderings, the mix of the brighter blacks with the grayer ones works well. The mix of the different shades of black makes the design of the quilt more interesting. (See page 44 for complete directions to make this quilt.)

Supplies —

You Already Have What You Need

he most important component of a tee shirt quilt is, naturally, the tee shirts! They should all be washed before being made into a quilt. Chances are that you will be working with tee shirts that have been laundered many times, but if you have new shirts that have never been washed, go ahead and run them through the laundry at least once. That way, if your quilt requires laundering in the future, you won't run the risk of having one tee shirt that shrinks when all the others don't, or one that bleeds color onto the quilt.

Incidentally, do not be too concerned that faded tee shirts will not work well in your quilt. The motif takes on a different quality when it is cut away from the tee shirt and sewed into the quilt. You may be surprised at how attractive even a pale, worn motif can appear in the final quilt.

This quilt was inspired by author tours that the maker of the quilt and its recipient took through Mississippi, one behind the other, a day apart. Mary Elizabeth was promoting *Mississippi Quilts,* and Marlin (Bart) Barton was promoting *A Dry Well.* Mary would find, as she arrived at each location, that Bart had been at the same place the day before. The two of them finally caught up with one another in the lobby of the Peabody Hotel in Memphis. Along the way, Mary had decided to commemorate their successful book tours by making each of them a quilt, and she began collecting tee shirts at each of their stops. Later she filled in with shirts from Bart's home state of Alabama, the two universities he attended, and the jazz club where he met his wife. He and his bride honeymooned in New York City shortly after the World Trade Center destruction, and tee shirts commemorating their trip are also included.

FABRIC STABILIZER

You will need only one specialized product for making your tee shirt quilt—a fabric stabilizer.

A stabilizer is necessary because tee shirts are made from stretchy knit fabrics, but when they are used in a quilt, they *must behave like non-stretchy woven fabric* (like the cotton fabrics we quilters normally use for our projects). The appropriate stabilizer for tee shirt quilts is fusible interfacing, a fabric that is coated on one side with heat-sensitive resins. When you iron the resin-coated side of the interfacing to the wrong side of the tee shirt, a bond forms between the two fabrics which eliminates the comfy stretchy quality that is wonderful in a tee shirt but unsuited for a quilt.

You can choose from two kinds of stabilizers: woven and non-woven. The non-woven is more generally available; one that is widely distributed to fabric shops is Pellon Fusible Nonwoven Interfacing, which comes in two different weights. Both weights are available in black and in white. *Be sure to get the heavier weight,* as a lightweight one is not strong enough to do the job. It cannot withstand even mild stress, such as someone sitting on the quilt, without stretching or tearing, which would of course allow the knit to return to its stretchy state.

The second type of fusible interfacing is woven and is carried in some quilt shops as well as in most general fabric stores. It is available in only one weight, but in two colors, black and white. White will work just fine for all your tee shirts, even those with a black background. If you have a large quantity of black tee shirts, you might want to use black fusible interfacing, although it certainly is not necessary.

Note: The resins from fusible interfacings do not stick to the sewing machine needle, nor do they harm the machine in any way. Garment-makers have been using these interfacings for years with no problems.

ANOTHER HELPFUL FUSIBLE

Fusible materials are big time-savers and have become an essential part of a quilter's supply cabinet. In addition to fusible interfacing, you should have a supply of fusible web. Fusible web can be purchased in pre-cut packets or by the yard. It comes attached to a paper liner, which allows it to be ironed onto one fabric surface, then to another after the paper liner is peeled away. It is the ideal material for adhering a fabric label to the back of a quilt.

RULERS

Basically, you need rulers that will allow you to easily cut around the printed motif on your tee shirts. A 15-inch or 16½-inch acrylic square ruler, such as those made by Omnigrid® or Quilter's Rule®, is going to be the most useful. You can, of course, use smaller square

"A Writerly Quilt," made by Mary Elizabeth Johnson, Montgomery, Alabama, 2004. Quilted by Angela Taylor, New Traditions Machine Quilting, Birmingham, Alabama. (The alphabet is quilted into the narrow navy border.) 72" X 80". Collection of Bart Barton and Rhonda Goff-Barton, Montgomery, Alabama.

"Our Precious Planet," made by the author in Fairhaven, Massachusetts in 2003. Quilted by Cathy Franks, Carmel, Indiana. 41" X 44". Collection of the author, Indianapolis.

rulers, but if you use tee shirts with large motifs, the larger square makes your job much easier.

If, however, you are using a very small or child's tee shirt, a smaller square ruler, such as the 12½-inch or the 9½-inch, may be easier to fit on the smaller motifs.

CUTTING MAT AND ROTARY CUTTER

It is essential that your cutting mat be large enough to accommodate your tee shirts. A 35-inch by 23-inch is a good size, as is a 17-inch by 11-inch. The smaller mat is easier to slip inside a tee shirt, in the event that you want to cut motifs from both the back and the front of the tee shirt. The size of your rotary cutter is your choice; just make sure to put a sharp new blade on before beginning your tee shirt quilt.

SEWING MACHINE AND GENERAL SEWING SUPPLIES

Each time you begin a new project, you should clean the lint out of your sewing machine, including the bobbin mechanism, and insert a new, sharp needle. Size 80 and 90 general sewing needles work well.

Pre-fill several bobbins before you begin sewing. It can be annoying to have to stop and re-fill a bobbin in the middle of a seam. It's much easier to have one ready to go and just pop it in.

No special thread is required. Generally, a light-to-medium gray or beige works well with most colors, and black works best with black fabrics and tees. If you're working with a mixture of black and other colors, a gray bobbin thread is generally the best choice, as it is unobtrusive.

FABRICS

At the beginning of each new class, the students' greatest concern is selecting the fabric for the quilt's sashing and borders. This is especially true when a student's assortment of tee shirts includes many different colors, which is most often the case. Such a situation calls for a fabric audition, which is great fun. Ideally, the audition takes place in a quilt shop.

Before beginning the fabric audition, decide which colors in your tee shirts are the ones you want to emphasize in the quilt. Then, head over to the section of the shop that features those colors and hold a couple of your chosen motifs up to several different bolts. When you find a few fabrics you like, take the potential candidates to a quiet spot in the shop. An empty classroom is ideal, especially if you can push two tables together, giving you enough space to unroll a couple yards from the bolt. Spread the fabric out, then place a row or so of the tee shirt motifs onto the fabric, leaving spaces between them to represent sashing. (If you have not cut the motifs out yet, fold the shirts to highlight the area you will use in the quilt.)

Do not immediately discard tee shirts with rips or tears in them, even if the damage is near the motif. There are ways to disguise those holes. (See page 30.)

Stand back from your layout, even across the room if possible, in order to see how the fabric and tee shirts work together. Distance gives a better perspective than close quarters. Audition each of your candidates until you find the one that is right for the sashing.

Next, audition your border fabrics by unrolling a couple yards, then positioning the fabric on the table around the outer edge of the block/sashing arrangement. Try a few different choices; it's amazing, but the correct choice will practically shout at you, "I'm perfect." You may also discover that you want to use more than one border.

If the shop's classroom is not available, see if you can find a quiet corner to lay your arrangement out on the floor. Often other shoppers will happen by and offer suggestions as well as support. (Aren't quilters wonderful!) Shop employees can be great sources of suggestions, and, if you are not there on a sale or other busy day when staff is overwhelmed with customers, they are usually happy to be of assistance.

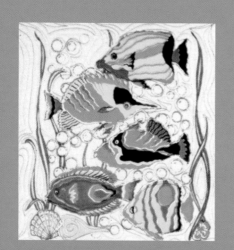

Personal experience has taught me that the color of the sashing should be of the same character as the tee shirt motifs: brights go best with brights, for example; pastels with pastels; muted tones with muted tones. The pattern of the sashing fabric should generally not outshine the motifs; you can almost always count on a print that reads like a solid to be a winner. Examples are mottled, subdued prints, tone-on-tones, and hand-dyed fabrics (or those that look like hand-dyes).

For the main border, the all-time favorite is a fabric that goes with the theme of the quilt, whether sports, music, travel, or whatever. A bold print can be very effective, especially if it incorporates most of the colors found in the tee shirt motifs. Darker borders seem to provide the best frame for the quilt. And, be certain to keep the quilt's recipient in mind; a boy won't appreciate a floral design as much as he will a plaid or abstract—anything that's less feminine than flowers!

QUILT BATTINGS

With the broad array of quilt battings available on the market today, it can be difficult to know which one to choose. The best general advice I can give you is to select a good quality batting, because after all, you are making a special quilt and you want it to last. Your final choice of batting should be determined by how you are going to quilt the piece (hand-tie or machine-stitch? rows of stitches close together or far apart?); fiber content (cotton, cotton/polyester, polyester, wool, or silk?); and thickness of the batting (thin, medium, or thick like a comforter?).

If you are going to machine-quilt the piece, I recommend a thin to medium weight batting in cotton or a cotton/polyester blend. Read the package information to learn the maximum distance between rows that quilting can be done. Some packaging will say "quilting up to three to four inches apart;" others will go up to eight, and even twelve, inches apart. The batting that allows rows to be eight to twelve inches apart is the correct choice if you plan to quilt sparsely. There are many more batting choices if you plan to quilt more densely.

Here are a few of my favorite brands: Hobbs Heirloom® 80% cotton/20% polyester batting, which can be quilted up to three and a half inches apart; Quilters Dream Cotton® and Warm and Natural® cotton can be quilted as far apart as eight inches; Mountain Mist® Cream Rose (also White Rose) are 100% cotton and can be quilted up to six inches apart; Quilter's Dream® Blend Batting is 70% cotton/30% polyester and can be quilted up to twelve inches apart.

If you are going to tie (tuft) the quilt, the filling I recommend is not a batting at all, but a fusible polyester fleece. The fusible battings now being manufactured are NOT appropriate for tied quilts, because they sometimes become undone. Fusible fleece by Pellon® is the one to get; it provides a permanent fuse. The fleece is thin; if you prefer additional loft, you might use more than one layer of fleece, fusing each in turn, following the manufacturer's instructions.

MISCELLANEOUS USEFUL ITEMS

Fabric pens: Now found in quilt shops and some fabric stores, the ink in these pens is permanent, does not fade, and is washable. The pens are available with points that range from very fine to a flexible tip that allows broad strokes, depending on the amount of pressure you apply. The flexible tip functions in much the same way as a brush.

Freezer paper: Once found only in the kitchen, freezer paper has shown itself to be useful in the sewing room because the waxy side is heat-sensitive. Cut to the required size and shape, it is a handy aid to appliqué. It is a great stabilizer for fabrics on which you wish to write, such as quilt labels. Keep a quantity on hand.

WHAT SIZE DO I MAKE MY QUILT?

The overall size of your quilt is one of the factors that determine the amount of fabric and batting you will need. The other primary influences on your supply list are the number of decorative details you decide to include, but more about that in the next chapter.

Standard measurements for mattresses and recommended measurements for quilts for each.

	MATTRESS	QUILT
Crib	27" X 52"	45" X 60"
Twin	39" X 75"	59" X 85"
Full	54" X 75"	74" X 85"
Queen	60" X 80"	80" X 90"
King	76" X 80"	96" X 96"

12

Back

Front

Techniques

Getting Down to Business

The first thing you must do, once you have made your final selection of tee shirts and washed them, is cut the decorative motifs out of the shirts. You should carefully examine each shirt to determine where the motifs are located. Many tee shirts have designs printed on the back of the shirt as well as the front, and you may want to use both of them. Others have a motif on only one side, either the back or the front. Others may have smaller motifs on a pocket or a sleeve that you may want to incorporate in some way.

Once you have examined all your shirts, separate them into three piles: one with motifs on both sides, one with motifs on one side, one with smaller motifs in addition to the main one(s).

CUTTING THE TEE SHIRTS

Method I. For a Tee Shirt with Motif on One Side Only

Place the tee shirt, motif side up, on your cutting mat. Center the acrylic square ruler over the motif, and using the rotary cutter, cut around the motif, going through the entire shirt, front and back. *This is the quickest and easiest method to remove the motif from the shirt.*

Simply laying the tee-shirt flat on your cutting board and cutting through both layers, front and back, is the easiest way to remove the part you want.

Step 1. Carefully center acrylic square over the shirt motif. Note that side margins are generous, and are equal, as are top and bottom margins.

Step 2. Using rotary cutter, cut around all four sides of acrylic square.

Step 3. The cut-out motif has wide margins on all four sides.

Method II. For A Tee Shirt With Motifs On Both Front And Back

Slip your cutting mat inside the tee shirt, with one motif facing up. It makes no difference which side—back or front—you do first. Center the acrylic square ruler over the motif. Using the rotary cutter, cut the motif out.

Remove the cutting mat, turn the tee shirt over, and re-insert the mat into the remains of the tee shirt. Center the acrylic square ruler over the second motif and cut it out with the rotary cutter.

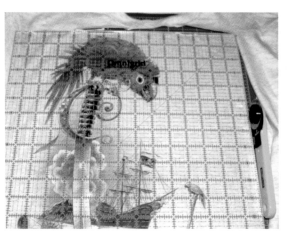

Step 1. Slip the cutting board *inside* the tee shirt. Center acrylic square over the desired motif, and cut with rotary cutter along all four sides of ruler.

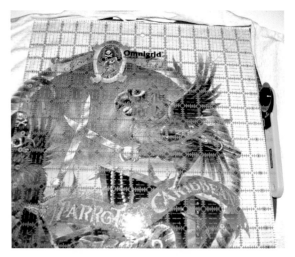

Step 2. Cut the motif from the back of the tee-shirt, following the method used for the front.

Method III. Cutting a Small Motif from a Sleeve or Pocket

If any of the shirts you're working with happen to have a small, supporting motif on a sleeve or a pocket, you should cut it out for possible use in your project. You never can tell, but it may turn out to be just the creative touch you need. (Keep it until the quilt is completely finished and you are sure you have no use for it. Once it's discarded, it's gone for good.)

Cut the entire section containing the small logo away from the shirt. If it's on a sleeve, cut the sleeve off. If it's on a pocket, cut the pocket out. Give the motif as much margin as possible.

An alternative method is to cut the tee shirt apart with scissors along the shoulder and sleeve seams, then down the sides. You can then separate the shirt into front and back, and cut out the motif using the acrylic square ruler, rotary cutter, and mat.

Step 1. Alternatively, you can cut the tee-shirt apart along the shoulders, sleeves, and sides, so that the back and front are completely separated from one another.

Step 2. You can then individually remove the motifs from the front and back.

Measure each motif to determine the largest and smallest blocks it could make.

IMPORTANT

Be careful not to

pull or stretch the

motifs while you

are working

with them.

FROM A TEE SHIRT MOTIF TO A QUILT BLOCK

Once you've removed all the motifs from all the tee shirts, you have the beginnings of your quilt blocks. You will sort and size and play with the blocks until you are pleased with the overall flow of the design. Sometimes surprises are waiting for you—a block might end up in a different size or place than you had imagined. Follow these steps to be sure you get the most out of your motifs-turned-quilt-blocks.

1. Measure the motifs. One by one, go through the blocks in order to determine the possible maximum and minimum sizes for each. Use the acrylic square to measure, and be sure to include a $\frac{1}{4}$ inch seam allowance on all sides of the block.

Label each motif with both maximum and minimum sizes by writing directly onto a corner of the motif with a permanent marking pen, or by pinning on a scrap of paper with the measurements.

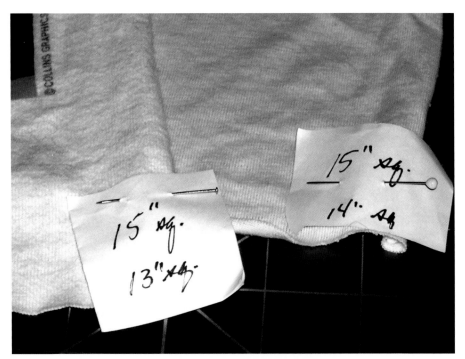

Mark each motif with its maximum and minimum sizes.

2. Plan the rough layout for your blocks. Separate the blocks according to their size possibilities. When that is done, look through each stack of blocks with the following question in mind. Do you have enough blocks of the same size to make one row (either horizontal or vertical) in the quilt?

In examining the blocks, you may find that you could, for example, make a row of 14-inch blocks, if only you had another couple of blocks. You would then look in the next-size-up stack to see if there are any whose minimum size could be 14 inches. If you're lucky and find some, then move them to your 14-inch stack. Do not, however, trim them to size quite yet.

Continue sorting and planning your rows, with the understanding that the rows don't all have to be the same size, although the blocks within each row must be. You can alternate a tall row with a short row if you want. You can also make vertical rows rather than horizontal rows, but horizontal rows seem somehow to be easier.

When you have sorted the blocks, lay them out in rows on your design wall or on a floor or bed. Try to choose a location where the block layout can remain undisturbed for a day or so.

As you go about your daily activities, make it a point to pass by your layout frequently. Pause to re-arrange any blocks that you think will look better in a different location. You may find that the color balance will be better, or the harmony is improved if you place a different motif next to another. When you are satisfied with the arrangement, it is time to size the blocks and apply stabilizer.

NOTE

If you find that you don't have enough motifs of the same size to make a row, you may elect to frame the motifs with fabric to enlarge the block to the size you need. See "Framing Blocks Of Uneven Sizes And Shapes." (Page 24)

18

First, though, make a quick snapshot of the layout. A Polaroid® or digital camera is ideal, but you can also use a regular camera.

As you remove each block from the design wall, pin on a note as to its location: Row 1, Block A; Row 1, Block B, etc.

3. Size the blocks. Once you've decided on the size you want each block to be, you must trim them to that size. However, a good pressing of each block comes first.

Lay each block face-side down on the ironing surface, smooth out all wrinkles, and carefully press the block flat. You may want to use a press cloth. Press with an up-and-down motion; lift the iron away from the block, move it to the next position, and set it down flat. Be careful not to move the iron around the surface of the block, as that may cause stretching and become distortion. Repeat the lift-and-press technique until entire block is wrinkle-free; you don't want wrinkles permanently fused to the stabilizer.

You may notice that two opposite sides of the block have a tendency to curl, but do not worry about that—just press the block smooth. (All knit fabrics tend to curl along the cut edges.)

The next step is to size your blocks. In this initial sizing, you will cut the blocks *one-half inch longer and one-half inch wider* than the finished size. This allows one-fourth inch seam allowances all around.

Lay each smooth, flat block onto the cutting mat. Place the large acrylic square over it, and cut it to the desired size plus one-fourth inch all around.

Press each tee shirt block before sizing it; don't be concerned if the edges try to curl.

IMPORTANT

Be careful not to pull or stretch

the motifs while you are

working with them.

NOTE

If your tee shirt blocks are squares, you need to determine which direction of both the tee shirt block and the stabilizer has the most stretch. (The stabilizer will be stretchier in one direction, just as the tee shirt block will be.) Select one tee shirt block and its matching piece of stabilizer. Give both the block and the stabilizer a slight pull, horizontally and vertically, to see which direction of each is the stretchiest. You will want to be sure to pair the most stable direction of the stabilizer to the most-stretchy direction of the tee-shirt block. (This applies only to blocks that are square, unless you work it out before you cut the stabilizer. If, for example, you are using a rectangular shape, and the longest direction of the tee shirt block is the stretchiest, you would cut the stabilizer so its length was placed on the least stretchy direction.)

4. Stabilize the blocks. You may want to review the information given on page 6 regarding fabric stabilizers that work well with tee shirts. Whatever your choice of stabilizer, you will probably buy it by the yard. The non-woven stablizers come with directions for the product's use printed onto thin plastic sheeting that is wound by the yard onto the bolt. The woven stabilizers do not come with instructions; set the iron to a cotton setting and follow the directions given here. The stabilizer, whether woven or non-woven, needs no preparation, such as washing, before being used.

Place the resin-coated side of the stabilizer face down on your cutting mat, and, using your acrylic square and rotary cutter, cut a piece of stabilizer for each tee shirt block. Same size, same shape.

Working on your ironing surface, place the tee shirt block face down and smooth it flat, unrolling any curled edges. Place the stabilizer fusible-side down onto the tee shirt block, making sure the stretchier direction of the stabilizer goes in the opposite direction from the block.

Using the iron in the up-and-down motion, fuse the stabilizer to the tee shirt block. Move the iron slowly over the surface of the stabilizer. Remember that the tee shirt blocks are knits, so be careful to keep them from stretching while you are fusing. Reinforce the fusing at the four corners by ironing over them a second time.

Apply stabilizer to all the blocks of your quilt.

Fuse the stabilizer to the wrong side of the tee shirt block, going over the corners a second time.

"Memories" made by the author in Indianapolis, 2005. 41" X 41". Collection of the author.

This quilt is an example of one in which the blocks are the same size, and they are set side-by-side on the diagonal. (See page 50 for complete directions to make this quilt.)

Tricks of the Trade

O nce you have your motifs ready to go, the fun really starts. You begin working with additional design elements that will enhance your selection of motifs and contribute to the overall appearance of the quilt. You make decisions about the size you want your finished quilt to be, and, frankly, about how much more effort you are willing to put into the quilt. If you are in a hurry and only need a small quilt, you can sew the blocks together into rows, then sew the rows together, add a border, and your top is finished.

However, this book is about making *fabulous* tee shirt quilts, so I am sure that you will want to take a few additional steps with each of your own projects to make sure they are really beautiful! Study the following suggestions to get your own ideas sparking.

"Coast to Coast," made by the author in Indianapolis in 2006. 44" X 60". Collection of the author.

The motifs are from trips to the West and East coasts—California and Florida. Notice that the final selection of frame colors is not exactly the same as those in the audition. That is what the audition is about—selecting and refining possibilities.

PLANNING THE FINAL LAYOUT

Same size blocks set side by side: The easiest quilt to make is the one in which the motif blocks are the same size, set side-by-side, with no further procedures done to them. However, easy does not always mean interesting, and we want our quilts to be interesting. That is why I added corner triangles to the five motifs in "Memories." (See page 20.) The corner triangles not only add punches of color, they frame and enhance each motif and make it possible for the blocks to be set on the diagonal.

Framing same-size blocks: An alternative to adding corner triangles to same-size blocks is to frame them with fabric. Almost all blocks are improved by the addition of framing, no matter the motif, the shape, or the size. Even the distinctive images of "The Billy Joel Wall Hanging" (pages 25, 42, 48) are well-served by being framed in colors chosen to coordinate with the details of the motifs.

The selection of the color for your fabric frames is important. It should highlight the design of the motif within the block. Frames can be all the same color, as in "The Billy Joel Wall Hanging", or they can be of many different colors, as in "Suzanna's Memory Quilt", (page 24) or "Precious Planet" (pages 8, 42, 59). I often audition different frame colors on my design wall.

Step 1. I wanted to use these six tee shirt motifs to tell a particular story, although their styles and colors were very different. A black design wall provided the background for a potential layout for the motifs. (All motifs have been pressed, stabilized, and trimmed to size.)

Step 2. After deciding that framing each motif with a variety of solid colors would pull them together into a whole, I began auditioning different possibilities by pinning strips into place on the design wall.

"Suzanna's Memory Quilt", made by Jane Lee in Indianapolis in 1995. 60" X 86". Collection of Suzanna Lee, Chicago, Illinois.

The many tee shirts used in this quilt tell the story of Suzanna's growing up in southeast Asia. Notice how framing has been used to create horizontal rows consisting of motifs in many different sizes and shapes.

Framing blocks of uneven sizes and shapes—two methods: It seems to be the nature of tee shirt quilts that the motif blocks turn out to be many different sizes and shapes. However, because you need blocks of the same size to make rows, you will use framing to build each block up to the size and shape required. The framing will also serve to highlight the motifs in the block, so color and design should be carefully chosen, with thought to how they contribute to overall design of the quilt.

When our son approached us to ask permission to attend his first concert, his dad and I cringed, thinking of heavy metal rock bands of the time like "Nine Inch Nails." We asked who he wanted to see, and when he said, "Billy Joel," we sighed with relief! The tee shirt Tevlin bought that night became a favorite, and he wore it until he outgrew it. It was the knowledge of what this particular souvenir meant to my son that inspired me to make this, my very first tee shirt wall hanging!

(See page 48 for complete directions to make this quilt.)

"Billy Joel Wall Hanging," made by the author in Indianapolis in 1994. 26" X 47".
Collection of Tevlin Schuetz, Indianapolis.

**Method 1. When blocks
are different sizes**, the framing
strips must be cut wider for the
smaller blocks and narrower for
larger blocks in order to make
all the blocks in a row the same
size. Determine the size of the
largest block in the row, then
measure all the other blocks to
decide how wide the framing
will need to be to bring each
block up to that size. Be sure to
include seam allowances on the
framing strips.

You may want to do all the
measuring and cutting at once,
or you may want to cut and
frame one block at a time.

*"Brian's T-Shirt Quilt" made by Anita Harden in Indianapolis in 1993. 66"
X 88". Collection of Brian Weir-Harden, Bloomington, Indiana.*

This quilt was built in vertical rows; frames of various widths and
lengths, along with squares and rectangles of African-themed fabric,
have been used to make all the blocks in each row the same size.
The tee shirts were favorites from the collection her son had in high
school, and Anita made the quilt for him as a high school graduation
gift. Twelve years later, Brian wrote about what the quilt means to
him: "When I first received the quilt, I was impressed by how
skillfully my mother coordinated my old tee shirts into something so
creative and well-made. Now, having had the quilt for so many years,
it has become a symbol of my mother's limitless capacity to love and
care unconditionally."

"Our Travels", made by the author in Indianapolis in 1996. 39" X 44". Collection of M.J. Schuetz, Jr., Indianapolis.

A square block and four rectangular blocks have been framed in the "Log Cabin" method so they can be sewn together to make rows. (See page 54 for complete directions to make this quilt.)

Method 2. When the motif blocks are not only different sizes, but are different shapes, multiple frames may be the answer. In order to combine the five completely different motifs of "Our Travels," I framed each block using a modified "Log Cabin" approach to bring each block up to the size and shape I needed to make a row. I made two little patchwork blocks to fill in the center row, although I could have inserted squares of fabric instead.

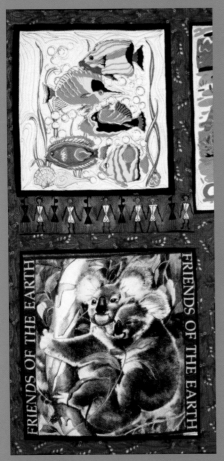

The top block in this panel from "Our Precious Planet" has been framed first with a simple black strip, then sashed on the right side and framed with a border print on the bottom. The lower block (with the Koala bears) has a very narrow black frame on all four sides. A sashing strip joins it to the block above, forming a vertical row of two blocks. A row of sashing has been stitched in place along the left-hand side of the row, in preparation for joining to the next segment of the quilt. Sashing is most important in making the five blocks of this little quilt fit together into a beautiful whole. (See page 59 for complete directions to make this quilt.)

Sashing: It looks very much like framing, but sashing actually serves a different purpose. It is used to link parts of the quilt together. It joins blocks to one another, and once the blocks have become rows, sashing can be used to join rows to one another.

The use of sashing in a quilt is strictly optional. It is a marvelous way to add color and pattern to a quilt, and it can be the unifying element that brings together into a harmonious whole all those dissimilar motifs.

Sashing also allows you to make the quilt larger. You choose the width of the sashing according to the size you want your finished quilt to be. Sashing and borders are the two elements that can be manipulated to get your quilt to the size you want.

Sashing gives you a perfect opportunity to add design elements to the quilt. The makers of "Girl Scout Memories" incorporated many different fabrics and colors by randomly piecing their sashing strips. Careful examination reveals rows of light/dark squares, half-square triangles, bars, and "Flying Geese."

A vertical row of "Flying Geese" repeats the colors found in the tee shirt motifs and their borders.

The "Geese" also fly horizontally. Notice the narrow row of half-square triangles used as vertical sashing, and, in the lower left corner of the photo, the "Bars" that make another vertical sashing.

"Girl Scout Memories," made by Carol Greenham Victory and Sharon Lehman in Houston, Texas in 1999. 65" X 65". Collection of Jennifer Victory Newberg, Indianapolis.

Jennifer is Carol's daughter and collected the tee shirts during her twelve years as a Girl Scout.

Using those small motifs:

As you plan the layout for your blocks, you may find that you need a little accent in a certain place. There may be too much background in a particular block, or the perfection of a block may be marred by a spot, tear, or hole. That is the perfect location for one of your small motifs.

You can use a small motif as the center of a quilt block, like a "Variable Star" or a "Nine Patch." Plan ahead so that the finished quilt block will be the size you need to fit into a row.

You can also cut a small motif out, stabilize and cut it to size, then simply place it where you want it on your quilt top and satin-stitch in place, making sure to adjust the width of the stitch to cover all raw edges. (Turning under the raw edges results in too much bulk.)

A small worn place in one of the integral tee shirts for my "Coast to Coast" quilt required some creative repair.

Another tee shirt provided a perfect motif to cover the little blemish.

The repair emphasized that this motif represented the Atlantic coast, since it added "Florida" to "Myrtle Beach!"

Using a single tee shirt: You can make a one-block wall hanging or pillow top out of a special tee shirt. The motif can be treated simply, as in the "Ottawa, Canada" pillow, or it can be set into a more complicated background, as in "Sawtooth Star."

"Ottawa, Canada," made by Carol Greenham Victory, Indianapolis. Collection of Jennifer Newberg, Indianapolis.

This tee shirt contained four motifs emblematic of the Canadian province, making it a perfect choice for a single-block project.

"Sawtooth Star," made by the author in Indianapolis, 2005. 38" X 38"; collection of Dr. Jay Schuetz, Decatur, Illinois.

(See page 63 for complete directions to make this quilt.)

*"Stars with a Tee," made by Deborah Oliver in Jefferson City, Tennessee, in 2000. 80" X 80".
Collection of the maker.*

Finishing the Quilt

he motif blocks have been framed, sashed, and assembled, providing you with a perfect opportunity to review your choice of border fabrics and make sure you are pleased with your earlier decisions. Once you have the border(s) on the quilt, you will put the layers of backing, batting and top together in preparation for quilting. Finally, the quilted piece must be bound and a label attached to the back. At various points along the way, you will want to check that the quilt is square, and fix it if it's not. Here are my suggestions for accomplishing these final procedures.

FRIENDS OF THE EARTH!

BORDERS

When you add borders to the quilt top, sew the two vertical (side) border strips on first, then the horizontal (top and bottom) strips. For multiple borders, follow this same procedure: sides first, then top and bottom. (This is not an iron-clad rule, and I sometimes put the top and bottom borders on before I do the sides. To my eye, however, it just seems better in most cases to put the side borders on first.)

For the vertical borders, measure the length of the quilt top through the center, from top to bottom. Decide on the width you think best (perhaps you decided on the width of the border(s) during your fabric auditions), and cut two strips of that width to equal the length of the quilt. Pin border strips onto the long raw edges of the quilt, right sides together, matching the center of the border strip to the center of the quilt and the ends of the border to the ends of the quilt. Position the quilt top under the needle with the border up and the quilt top down, and sew the two together with a $\frac{1}{4}$" seam. The feed dogs will ease in any surplus length that may occur along the outer edges of the quilt top, as long as it's not excessive. Repeat for the other vertical border. Press seams toward the border.

For the horizontal borders, measure across the center of the quilt top and cut two border strips in your chosen width to that length. Pin and stitch as for the vertical borders.

Repeat until you have sewn all your borders onto the quilt.

Look over the back of the quilt top and cut off any hanging threads. Lightly press the entire top.

SQUARING THE QUILT TOP

I recommend that you square your work at several different stages during construction. 1. Square each block as it is made and pressed. 2. Square the top after all the blocks have been sewn together with sashing and pressed—before any borders are on. 3. Square a final time after all the borders are on and the top is completed and pressed. By the time the top is quilted, it should be in good shape and require no further squaring, but if it is a bit off, it can be squared before the binding is applied.

To square a piece of work, no matter what size, carefully take horizontal and vertical measurements in three different places: through the middle and on both outside edges. The three measurements should be the same or very close. If there is a slight variance, make a note of exactly where it occurs.

A large square acrylic ruler is invaluable for squaring up the corners of the quilt. Place the quilt on a cutting mat and position the square ruler in the corner, aligning the edges of the ruler with one horizontal edge and one vertical edge of the fabric as exactly as possible. Holding the ruler firmly in place, trim away any small excess of fabric along both horizontal and vertical edges of the corner. Repeat for all four corners of the work.

Next, use long acrylic rulers to cover the distance between the squared corners; align the rulers as closely as possible with the edge, using the just-squared portions as guides to placement. Cut away any excess fabric. Repeat for all four sides of the work.

Measure again through the vertical center and along both sides. If there is still a difference in the three measurements, go back and trim away where needed to make the two sides the same length. It may be best to take half of the difference from the top of the piece and the other half from the bottom. Repeat for the horizontal direction of the piece.

SQUARING THE QUILT TOP

1. Square each block as it is made and pressed.

2. Square the top after all the blocks have been sewn together with sashing and pressed—before any borders are on.

3. Square a final time after all the borders are on and the top is completed and pressed.

ASSEMBLING THE QUILT/MACHINE QUILTING

1. Begin by "stitching in the ditch" around each block.

2. Consider enhancing individual motifs as suggested by each with free-motion quilting.

3. The sashing can be quilted or not.

4. Quilting the borders is usually not optional. They must be quilted.

5. Once quilting is finished, square the quilt once more.

ASSEMBLING THE QUILT/MACHINE QUILTING

Machine quilting is much easier than hand quilting to accomplish on tee shirt quilts, because it is difficult to get a hand needle through the motif and stabilizer once they are fused together.

To prepare for quilting, you must assemble the layers. Begin by spreading the quilt backing out flat on the floor or a large cutting surface, wrong side up. Spread the batting over the backing, smoothing it flat. Layer the quilt top over the batting. Baste the layers together, either by hand with needle and thread, with quilting safety pins, or a Quiltak® gun.

It is not my purpose to teach you to machine quilt in this small volume. However, I do have a few suggestions about how to go about it on your tee shirt quilt.

1. Begin by "stitching in the ditch" around each block; that is, place a row of straight stitching in the horizontal and vertical seamlines of the block; this will hold the three quilt layers together and will make any additional quilting easier to accomplish.

2. Next, consider enhancing individual motifs as suggested by each with free-motion quilting. If you don't know how to free-motion machine quilt, you can straight-stitch, keeping the feed dogs up. (Some machine quilters recommend dropping the feed dogs for machine-quilting, but I think you get better results leaving them up when straight-stitching.) A walking foot will make the job easier and yield better results than a regular presser foot. Plan the quilting design to be easily stitched on your sewing machine—think ahead to decide on how you will manage turns and curves.

You may conclude, if your blocks are not very large, that you do not need to quilt inside them at all. The batting you choose may also influence the amount of quilting you want to place within each block. (Refer to page 10 for information about battings.)

3. The sashing can be quilted or not, depending primarily on whether or not it is wide enough to contain a quilting design.

4. Quilting the borders is usually not optional, unless the border is a narrow one. Wide borders must be quilted, and can be a perfect showcase for a fancy stitching design, especially if they are made of a solid fabric. This is where a quilting stencil can be very handy, not only in choosing the right design, but in marking it. Your quilt shop is certain to have a wide selection of stencils and marking equipment. Personally, I prefer to mark with Chaco-Liner®, a chalk powder that rubs easily off the quilt when the quilting is finished. The powder comes in several different colors, making it easy to get one that shows up well on the border fabric.

5. Once quilting is finished, square the quilt once more. There should not be much variance in either length or width, and any small difference should be easily brought into line.

ASSEMBLING THE QUILT/TYING IT

An alternative to machine quilting is tying (also known as tufting). It is easy to do, and my method eliminates the need to apply a separate binding, because I make a knife-edge finish at the same time I assemble the three layers. I highly recommend that you use fusible fleece, because it helps to stabilize the entire quilt and it makes the process of securing the three layers together very simple.

1. Cut the fusible fleece to the same size as the quilt top. Place the quilt top right side down on the ironing board or ironing table, then layer the fleece, fusible side down, over the quilt top, matching all outside edges and smoothing away any wrinkles.

Follow the manufacturer's instructions to fuse the fleece onto the wrong side of the quilt top. If the quilt is a large one, you will find it easier to work section by section until the entire filling is fused onto the top. Square the quilt top/batting.

2. Now add the backing. Cut it to the same size as the quilt top/fleece. With the quilt top up and the fleece down, spread the backing, wrong side up, onto the quilt top. Align outer edges and smooth the layers flat. Pin or baste as you require.

3. Machine stitch, using a ¼" seam allowance, around all four sides of the quilt, leaving a 12" opening in the center of the bottom edge of the quilt.

4. Turn the quilt layers right side out by pulling them through the opening. Smooth, then press, the outer edges flat. Stitch the opening closed, either by hand with a slip-stitch, or by machine.

5. Now you are ready to tie the quilt. Lay it out and smooth it flat. Choose perle cotton or cotton yarn and a needle with a large eye. Begin by taking a stitch through all layers at the place where you want your first tie. Make a complete stitch, but do not cut the thread or yarn. Move to the next spot that you want a tie, and make another stitch. I don't measure ahead; I just "eyeball" the distance between ties, but you can use the design of the quilt top as a guide to placing the ties.

After you've covered the entire quilt, go back and cut the thread or yarn about halfway between each tie.

Take the two thread ends at each stitch and tie them into a square, or "surgeon's" knot: right over left, left over right. Cut thread ends to the approximate same length all over the quilt surface.

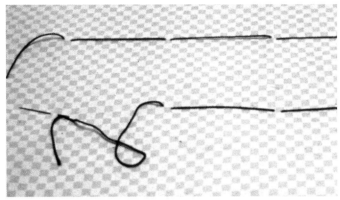

As you place your ties across the quilt, the result will look like a big long running stitch.

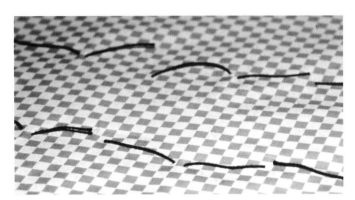

Clip halfway between all the stitches across the whole quilt, thereby making long thread ends.

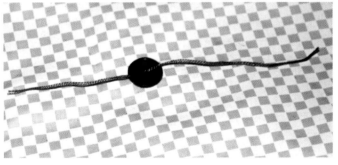

You can add beads, buttons, or bows to your ties. Make a square knot first as shown, then add desired decorative accent before you trim thread ends.

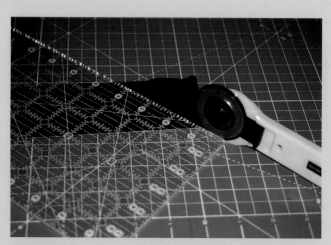

Photo A.

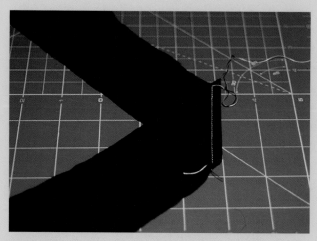

Photo B.

BINDING THE QUILT

If you do not use the method described previously, which yields a knife-edge finish for your quilt, you will need to bind the quilt. Binding is done after the quilting or tying is completed, and it finishes the edges of the quilt. Make certain the quilt is square before applying the binding.

1. Measure around all four sides of the quilt to determine the total length needed for the binding. Cut 2½"-wide strips across the width of the fabric until the required length is reached. Cut off selveges.

2. Line up an acrylic ruler's 45° angle mark with one long edge of the fabric strip, and cut both ends of the strip so they are on a perfect diagonal, going in the same direction. Repeat for all strips. (Photo A.)

3. Place right sides of two strips together, and stitch with a ¼" seam along the diagonal ends. Press seam allowances open. Repeat until all strips are joined to one another in a continuous length. Use a thread color that matches the fabric (The thread in the photo is a contrasting color for illustrative purposes only). (Photo B.)

4. Fold the strips wrong sides together so they are 1¼" wide. Press the strips to get a defined fold line.

5. Pin the binding to the right side of the quilt, beginning in the center of one side, and aligning the raw edges of the binding to the raw edges of the quilt, one side at a time. Curve the binding around the corners, allowing plenty of binding.

Leave a "tail" of at least ½" at beginning and end of binding. (Photo C.)

6. Stitch the binding in place with a ¼" seam, sewing the corners as follows.

(a) Stitch up to ¼" of the end of the seam and stop with the needle in the fabric; lift the presser foot. (Photo D.)

(b) Turn the work a quarter-turn. Lower the presser foot, and with the machine in reverse, stitch off the edge of the quilt. (Photo E.)

(c) Turn the work another quarter-turn and align the next stitching line with the ¼" guide. Fold the binding on the diagonal so that it resembles a mitered corner. Slowly resume stitching until the presser foot is back on the quilt and binding has been stitched in place. (Photo F.) Continue to the next corner at regular sewing speed, and repeat fold-and-stitch maneuver at remaining three corners.

7. At the end of stitching the binding on, line up the two ends of the binding and trim off any excess, leaving a ½" seam allowance on each end. Fold under the seam allowance on both ends, slip one end inside the other end, and stitch across the joining. (Photo G.)

8. Turn binding to the back of the quilt and hand stitch to the back.

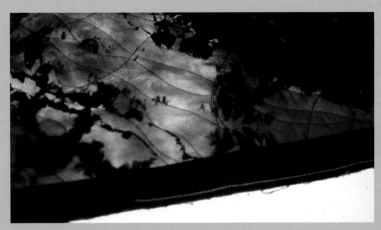

Photo C.

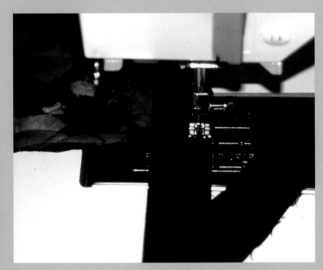

Photo D.

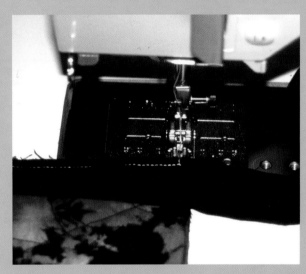

Photo E.

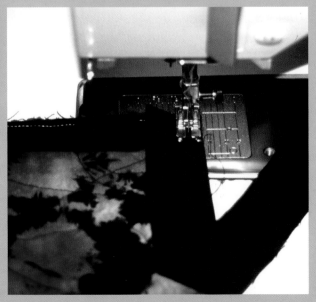

Photo F.

Photo G.

MAKING A DISTINCTIVE QUILT LABEL

If there is one thing we as quilters have learned, human memory alone does not serve to document a quilt's origins—that knowledge can be lost in just one generation. A label, permanently attached to the quilt, ensures that vital information about its origins will remain always with the quilt. Therefore, your quilt is not finished until you have tagged it with—at the very least—the name of the maker, along with the date and place it was made. You may add other information as you desire: for whom the quilt was made, the relationship of the maker to the quilt recipient, what the occasion was, and so on.

The quilt label should be made of fabric. You may want the convenience of using purchased fabric that has different styles of blank labels printed on it. You choose the label you want, cut it out, iron fusible web onto the wrong side (following the manufacturer's directions), write what you want on the label with a permanent fabric marking pen, and fuse it to the back of the quilt. Nothing could be simpler.

Another technique involves making your own label from a piece of white or light-colored fabric. A closely-woven fabric is best. Loose-weave fabrics, we have discovered in class, may allow the ink from the fabric pens to bleed.

Decide on the size you wish the finished label to be, and add seam allowances if you plan to sew the label on by hand (rather than fusing it in place with fusible web). Cut fabric and a corresponding piece of freezer paper to the desired size and shape (omit the seam allowances on the freezer paper). Iron the shiny side of the freezer paper onto the back of the fabric. Write, draw, or trace your desired message onto the right side of the fabric, using permanent fabric pens in as many colors as you choose. (A light box is helpful, but not necessary, for tracing a design. You can see through the fabric and freezer paper.)

If you are sewing the label on by hand, press the seam allowances to the wrong side of the label, using the edge of the freezer paper as a guide to a sharp edge. Remove the freezer paper. Stitch the label in place on the back of the quilt, using a blind stitch, a slip stitch, or a fancy embroidery stitch.

To fuse the label in place, cut out a piece of fusible web the same size and shape as the label. Following the manufacturer's instructions, fuse the web first to the back of the label, remove the paper backing, then fuse the label to the back of the quilt.

Computer software programs are now available for making quilt labels, and they are fun to use. You can play with different designs and quotes until you come up with a label that is exactly right for your particular quilt. Once designed, the label is printed onto a photo transfer fabric sheet that goes through the computer printer. Be certain that the fabric sheets you buy for your labels are certified as permanent and washable; if this is not stated in plain view on the package, choose another brand.

Hint: Always print your label design out on paper before going to fabric. Sometimes a design looks slightly different in print than on a computer screen. Make adjustments to the design before going to the more expensive fabric sheet.

Trim your computer label as necessary and attach it to the back of your quilt, either by hand or with fusible web.

Once your label is on the quilt, your one-of-a-kind memento is complete and ready to become a cherished keepsake for you or a loved one.

"Memories"
Caryl Schuetz
Indianapolis, Indiana
2005
A tee shirt quilt made with motifs from
Jay and Tev's favorite tee shirts

Your quilt is not finished until you permanently label it with the name of the maker as well as the date and place it was made. Other information may be included as you desire.

Caryl Schuetz
Woodhaven Studio
P.O. Box 68827 Traders Point
Indianapolis, Indiana 46268

Family's Core

Computer programs specifically for making quilt labels are fun to use and encourage you to fully document your work.

A FINAL WORD

If, in spite of all the fabulous information I have just provided for you to make your own beautiful tee shirt quilts, you prefer to get someone else to do it for you, here are two sources. Contact them directly for further information such as prices and exactly which services they provide.

42

The Black Quilt

Sawtooth Star

Memories

The Billy Joel Wall Hanging

Our Precious Planet

Our Travels

Step-by-Step

Directions for Six Fabulous Quilts

though I have revealed all the secrets to making a beautiful tee shirt quilt in the preceding chapters, my years of teaching have persuaded me that it is helpful to provide complete directions for someone's first project in a new technique. Consequently, I have chosen six of my quilts for step-by-step instructions. Each teaches a different lesson, and although you will not have the same tee shirts with which to work, you will easily see that you can freely adapt the techniques to your own stash of shirts.

The Black Quilt

Made by the author in Fairhaven, Massachusetts in 2004. Collection of M. J. Schuetz, Jr. Indianapolis, Indiana. Finished size: 58" X 70".

Although this is the easiest to make of all our projects, it does not sacrifice impact for simplicity. The sophisticated appearance of this quilt derives from the fact that all the tee shirt motifs are printed on black backgrounds and the supporting fabrics are carefully chosen to support a black color scheme. The motifs are set together side-by-side in four rows of three blocks. Although there is no sashing, a couple of the blocks were brought up to required size with the addition of strips of black fabric on two edges.

Materials

- Twelve tee shirt motif blocks that measure 14½" square or close to it. Retain any small motifs for possible use in filling in a background, mending a rip or tear, or adding detail.
- For first border: ½ yard fabric in a color that accents motifs
- For second border: 1⅔ yard of fabric in coordinating color
- For backing: 3½ yards of desired fabric
- Batting: 3½ yards
- Binding: ⅔ yard of desired fabric
- Black woven cotton as needed to enlarge blocks that do not measure 14½" square.

STEP 1. Cutting

Cut each tee shirt motif to 14½" X 14½;" stabilize all. (See "3. Size the blocks," page 18 and "4. Stabilize the blocks," page 19. Be certain to follow directions for adding seam allowances and for keeping the corners square. You will also need to follow the advice for working with square tee shirt blocks.)

For blocks that do not measure 14½" square (See diagram, page 47.), measure to determine how much must be added. Cut a strip of black cotton fabric to equal the length of the side to which the extension will be stitched and as wide as needed to make that direction of the block equal 14½", plus ½" for seam allowance. For example, if the block measures 11" X 11", the strip would be cut 11" X 4". Sew extender strip to block along the 11" side. To bring the second side up to size, cut another strip 14½" X 4". Align the 14½" edges of block and strip and stitch with a ¼" seam. Always press seam allowances toward strip.

For first border, cut eight 2"-wide strips across the width of the fabric. Trim selvages away, then sew strips together in pairs and press the seams open.

For the outer border, cut four 6½"-wide strips from the lengthwise direction of fabric.

STEP 2. Sewing

Sew three blocks together to make a row; repeat four times, then sew the rows together. Lightly press the quilt top, being careful not to place the iron on the logos. Square the top (See "Squaring the Quilt Top," page 35.)

To make the borders, first measure through the vertical center of your quilt; trim the strips for the side borders to equal this length. Pin side border strips in place, matching centers of borders to center of

In the bottom row, middle block, I used a small design to help fill a plain background. (Refer to "Using Those Small Motifs," page 30.)

quilt and ends of strip to outer edges of top; sew in place and press the seam allowances toward borders.

Measure through the horizontal center of the quilt, including the side borders; trim the strips for the top and bottom borders to this measurement. Pin top and bottom border strips in place, matching centers and ends. Sew in place; press seam allowances toward borders.

For backing: cut your yardage in half, selvage to selvage. Cut off selvages. Sew the two sections together so they go one above the other across the back of the quilt. Press.

STEP 3. Finishing

Follow the directions for "Squaring the Quilt Top" (page 35), "Assembling the Quilt/Machine Quilting" (page 36), and "Binding the Quilt" (page 38), or, alternatively, "Assembling the Quilt/Tying It" (page 37). Be certain to label your work (page 40).

Adapt the size of the blocks as needed

If the size of the blocks given in the preceding directions does not suit your needs, do not let that prevent your using this quilt plan. Simply cut blocks to the size you require, and adjust the amounts of fabric you buy for borders, backing, and binding accordingly.

Blocks That Do Not Measure 14½" Square

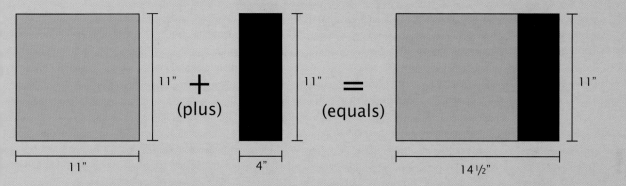

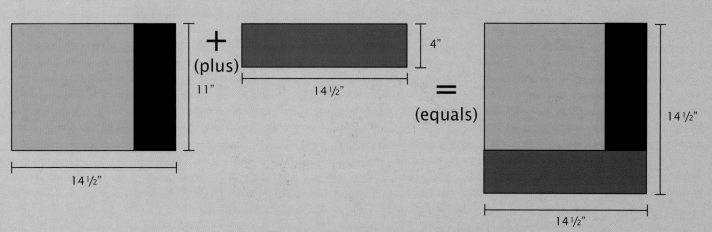

Cut a strip of black cotton fabric to equal the length of the side to which the extension will be stitched and as wide as needed to make that direction of the block equal 14½", plus ½" for seam allowance. For example, if the block measures 11" X 11", the strip would be cut 11" X 4". Sew extender strip to block along the 11" side. To bring the second side up to size, cut another strip 14½" X 4". Align the 14½" edges of block and strip and stitch with a ¼" seam. Always press seam allowances toward strip.

The Billy Joel Wall Hanging

Made by the author in Indianapolis, 1994. Collection of Tevlin Schuetz, Indianapolis. Finished size: 26" X 47".

This quilt demonstrates that a very attractive wall hanging can be made with only two motifs. Both came from the same Billy Joel concert tee shirt—one from the front and the other from the back.

I made the two motifs of the same size for my quilt, but your quilt could use two blocks of different lengths; just keep the widths the same. Any adjustments in the length of the blocks will require corresponding adjustments in the length of the sashing and border strips.

Of course, you may choose to use blocks of a completely different size from mine; you may also decide to use three, four, or even five blocks stacked on top of one another, especially if blocks are narrow. Just make sure that the length measurement of *the vertical sashing matches the combined length of the blocks plus horizontal sashing.* You will find that this plan for a vertical wall hanging is very versatile.

Materials

- Two tee shirt motifs (Note: I cut the tee-shirt into back and front sections before cutting out the motifs. (See "Cutting The Tee Shirts," page 14.)
- $\frac{1}{3}$ yard of fabric for sashing in a color that contrasts with or accents the motifs
- $\frac{2}{3}$ yard of fabric for border in a color that coordinates with motifs
- Backing: $1\frac{1}{2}$ yards
- Batting: $1\frac{1}{2}$ yards
- Binding: $\frac{1}{2}$ yard

STEP 1. Cutting

Cut each tee shirt motif to 16" wide by 18" long; stabilize both. (See "3. Size the blocks," page 18 and "4. Stabilize the blocks," page 19. Be certain to follow directions for adding seam allowances and for keeping the corners square.)

For the sashing, begin by cutting three 2" wide strips across the width of the fabric; divide them into lengths as follows:

for the sides: two $36\frac{1}{2}$" strips

to go between the two blocks: one 16" strip

for the top and bottom: two $18\frac{1}{2}$" strips

For the border, begin by cutting four $4\frac{1}{2}$" wide strips across the width of the fabric; divide them into lengths as follows:

for the sides: two 40" strips

for the top and bottom: two $26\frac{1}{2}$" strips

STEP 2. Sewing

Pin the 16" X 2" sashing strip to the bottom of the top block, matching centers and ends. Stitch in place with a $\frac{1}{4}$" seam. Sew the top edge of the bottom block to the sashing strip, again matching centers and ends. Press seam allowances toward the sashing.

Pin one $36\frac{1}{2}$" X 2" sashing strip in place on one side of motif unit, matching centers and ends. Stitch in place with a $\frac{1}{4}$" seam; press seam allowances toward sashing. Repeat for second side sashing.

Pin one $18\frac{1}{2}$" X 2" sashing strip to top of motif unit, matching centers and ends. Stitch in place with $\frac{1}{4}$" seam; press seam allowances toward sashing. Repeat for bottom sashing.

For the borders, repeat the sequence of sewing the side (40" X $4\frac{1}{2}$") borders in place first, then the top and bottom ($26\frac{1}{2}$" X $4\frac{1}{2}$") borders. Use a $\frac{1}{4}$" seam, and press seam allowances toward the sashing.

Lightly press the entire quilt top.

STEP 3. Finishing

Follow the directions for "Squaring the Quilt Top" (page 35), "Assembling the Quilt/Machine Quilting" (page 36), and "Binding the Quilt" (page 38), or, alternatively, "Assembling the Quilt/Tying It" (page 37). Be certain to label your work (page 40).

Memories

Made by the author in Indianapolis, 2005. Collection of the author. Finished size: 41" X 41".

A collection of tee shirts I had gathered on fun trips to California and the Caribbean with my husband inspired a wall quilt that makes a strong graphic statement. The motifs were wildly different from one another, and I decided to emphasize the difference by highlighting each motif with a coordinating accent fabric. I chose an aqua print to emphasize an aqua-and-red motif, then sewed a large triangle of it to each of the four sides of the square motif. If you study this quilt objectively, you will see that I have set squares of aqua, purple, green, red, and white into a red-white-and-gold background. Sounds risky, but I think it works, don't you?

I knew I could unify the different motifs by choosing a dynamic background fabric, and could provide further harmony by using the same fabric in the center of the quilt. Because I wanted this fabric to play such an important part, I decided to set the motifs on the diagonal, which allows a broad expanse of background.

Another detail that adds to the charm of this quilt is the way a couple of the motifs seem to grow into the blocks next to them. I saved the little extra bits of the design that extended beyond the square I cut for my motif, then after I sewed the rows of blocks together, I trimmed the bits to shape and fused them in place.

Materials

- Five tee shirt motifs (see "Cutting the Tee Shirts," pages 14-15)
- Fabric for side triangles: Fat quarters or ¼ yard cuts of four different fabrics (note that fabric of triangles in center block is same as background)
- Background (side and corner setting triangles) and corner triangles of center block: 1 yard
- Border: ½ yard
- Backing: 1⅓ yards
- Batting: 1⅓ yards
- Binding: ½ yard

STEP 1. Cutting

Cut each tee shirt motif to 9½" X 9½"; stabilize all. (See "3. Size the blocks," page 18 and "4. Stabilize the blocks," page 19. Be certain to follow directions for adding seam allowances and for keeping the corners square. You will also need to follow the advice for working with square tee shirt blocks.)

From each of the fat quarters, cut two 7½" squares; cut each in half on the diagonal to yield four triangles.

From the background fabric:

cut one 18¼" square, then cut it in half on both diagonals to make the setting triangles for the sides;

cut two 9⅜" squares, then cut each in half on the diagonal to make the setting triangles for the corners;

cut two 7½" squares, then cut each in half on the diagonal to make the corner triangles for the center square.

Border: Cut four 3½" wide strips across the width of the fabric.

This palm tree seems to grow up and out of its block. It does not matter if a bit of the motif is lost in cutting—the effect remains the same.

After fusing the topsails and pennants in place on the corner triangle, I straight-stitched along the edge of the raw-edge appliqué.

To make a quilt with a straight set

This style of quilt, which goes together very easily and quickly, is also a very good way to utilize small motifs, since each is enlarged by the addition of side triangles. The rows can be set together either with or without sashing.

If you cut your motifs out of the tee shirts in the regular manner, they will sit on the diagonal in the finished quilt, and will look just fine. However, if you want the motifs to sit straight in the finished quilt, you will need to cut them from the tee shirts on the diagonal. Simply place your square ruler over the motif so the corners are at the top and bottom and sides of the motif. Although the cutting itself is certainly no more difficult than in the regular method, you may find it a challenge to fit the entire motif into the diagonal cut. You will be led to the best decision—straight or diagonal—after experimenting with a few of your chosen motifs.

STEP 2. Sewing

Establish the center of each side of the tee shirt blocks by folding in half, first one way, then the other. Finger press the fold at the edge of the block, then open block up and place a pin at the fold. Establish the center of the long side of each fabric triangle by folding it in half to bring the outermost points together. Finger press on the fold, then mark with a pin.

Sew the fabric triangles to the motif blocks by placing right sides together, matching centers and aligning raw edges. Pin in place, and sew with a $\frac{1}{4}$" seam allowance. When one edge has been stitched, add the triangle to the opposite side, then add the two remaining triangles. Press seam allowances toward the triangles.

Follow theses steps for all 5 blocks, being sure to use the same fabric on the center block that will be used as the setting triangles for the quilt. Square up each block. (See "Squaring the Quilt Top," page 35.)

Sew the blocks together with the setting (background) fabric to make the rows. (See diagrams A & B, page 53.) Lightly press the quilt top, being careful not to place the iron on the logos. Square the top. (See "Squaring the Quilt Top," page 35.)

To make the borders, first measure through the horizontal center of your quilt; trim the strips for the top and bottom borders to equal this length. Pin top and bottom border strips in place, matching centers of borders to center of quilt and ends of strip to outer edges of top; sew in place and press the seam allowances toward borders.

Measure through the vertical center of the quilt and trim the strips for the side borders to this measurement. Pin side border strips in place, matching centers and ends. Sew in place; press seam allowances toward borders.

STEP 3. Finishing

Follow the directions for "Squaring the Quilt Top" (page 35), "Assembling the Quilt/Machine Quilting" (page 36), and "Binding the Quilt" (page 38), or, alternatively, "Assembling the Quilt/Tying It" (page 37). Be certain to label your work (page 40).

To make a larger quilt with a diagonal set

Plan your quilt by adding more blocks to make longer and wider rows. You can also add another border(s) or a wider border. Remember that each completed block that goes across will add another $17\frac{1}{2}$" to the width, and each one that add to the length will make your project $17\frac{1}{2}$" longer. (Example: 3 blocks across by 3 blocks down will make a $58\frac{1}{2}$" X $58\frac{1}{2}$" quilt. Cut a $6\frac{1}{2}$" wide border and the quilt will be $64\frac{1}{2}$" X $64\frac{1}{2}$" in size.) You should, of course, plan to purchase more fabric yardage for a larger quilt.

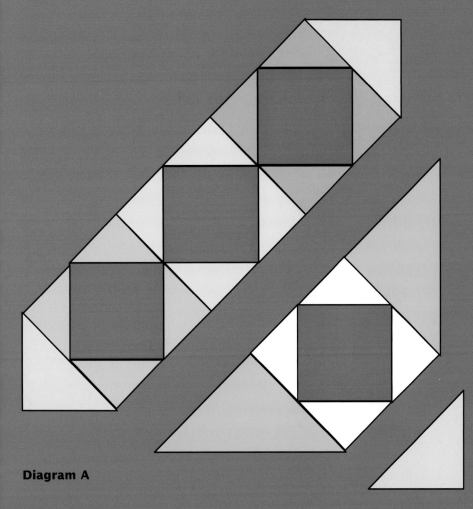

Sew the blocks together with the setting (background) fabric to make the rows.

Diagram A

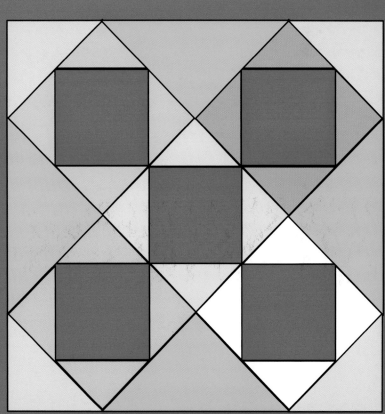

Diagram B

Our Travels

Made by the author in Indianapolis in 1996. Collection of M.J. Schuetz, Jr., Indianapolis. Finished size: 39" X 44".

Multiple frames applied in a *Log Cabin* fashion add a very interesting design element to this quilt. Because the framing strips are of different widths and colors, you have great freedom in cutting and sewing. The idea is to use the strips to build the blocks up to a particular height—one you have selected for the specific row in which the blocks will be placed. However, because the Log Cabin technique specifies that strips be sewn in rounds, you will also be adding to the width of the block as you build the height. Then, because a row of blocks is almost always going to be wider than it is tall, there will usually be a need to add extra strips at the sides of the blocks to attain the required width. You can make the rows different heights, but they must all be the same width. That is why you cut the Log Cabin strips in lots of widths and colors before you ever start sewing—to allow maximum flexibility.

In "Our Travels," I decided on three rows, and I decided to make the top row the tallest, the middle row the narrowest, and the bottom row almost as tall as the top one. The middle row contains only one tee shirt motif, in the center. To balance out that center motif, I paper-pieced two little sailboat blocks. I am not including a pattern for them, because you should choose an accent for these blocks that complements the tee shirt motifs you are using. Simple fabric squares will also work well, especially if they are of a print that supports the theme of the quilt.

Materials

- Five tee shirt motifs, two of which are vertical rectangles, three of which are horizontal rectangles (see "Cutting The Tee Shirts," pages 14-15)

- Two 5¼" pieced quilt squares or two 5¼" squares of solid fabric (Blocks 3 and 5)

- For the Log Cabin framing strips: Three different solid-color fabrics to complement and unify the tee shirt motifs—⅓ yard of each (mine are red, green, and burgundy)

- For seven Log Cabin framing strips plus the border: ⅔ yard of a fourth solid-color fabric (mine is purple)

- Backing: 1½ yards

- Batting: 1½ yards

- Binding: ½ yard

STEP 1. Cutting

Cut the two vertical rectangular motifs to the following sizes: 12½" wide by 13½" long (Block 1, upper left); and 9½" wide by 10" long (Block 6, lower left).

Cut the three horizontal rectangular motifs to the following sizes: 13½" wide by 10" long (Block 2, upper right); 14¾" wide by 6½" long (Block 4, center row); and 13¾" wide by 11¾" long (Block 7, lower right).

For the log cabin framing, cut strips across the width of the four colors of solid fabric in the following widths. Strips will be cut to the correct lengths as they are sewed in place.

From color A (green in "Our Travels"): two 1½"-wide strips.

From color B (red): one 1¾"-wide strip; one 1"-wide strip; one 2"-wide strip.

From color C (burgundy): one ¾"-wide strip; one 1½"-wide strip; one 2"-wide strip; and one 3¼"-wide strip.

From color D (purple): one 1¼"-wide strip; one 2"-wide strip; one 2½"-wide strip; and, for the border, four 4"-wide strips.

STEP 2. Sewing

Separate the motifs into the number of rows you desire—in *Our Travels,* I decided on three.

Next, decide on the exact depth and width you want each of the rows to be. Choose heights and widths that are different from any of your motifs so that you have the leeway to add several colorful strips to each motif. I decided to make the top row 15¼" tall, the bottom row 14" tall, and the middle row only 9¼" tall, and all rows would be 33" wide.

Because the strips are different widths and colors, you have lots of freedom in choosing how to build up the blocks. Begin by sewing a strip to one of the sides (usually the right side) of a motif and trim the strip even with the bottom edge of the motif. Then, add a strip of your choice to the bottom of the motif, matching the end of the new strip to the outer edge of the first strip. Continue until the entire block is surrounded by strips. Add a second round, or a partial second round, if needed. Square up each block as necessary when all strips have been added.

Use the Log Cabin strips to build all the blocks in one row to the same height and to the width you have decided to make the quilt. Then sew

Block Layout for "Our Travels"

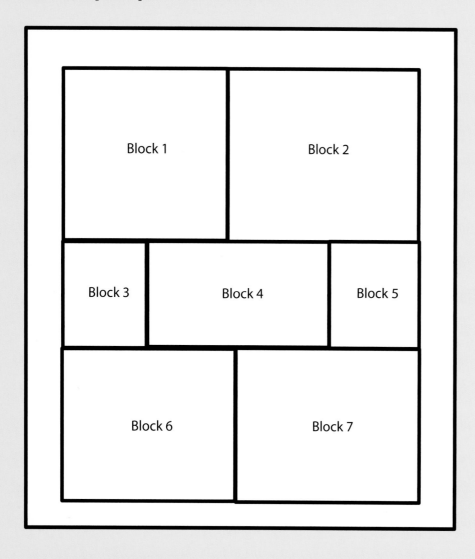

Block 1

Block 2

Block 3

Block 4

Block 5

Block 6

Block 7

the blocks together to make a row.

Make each row of the quilt by first making all the blocks the same height with the log cabin framing. Make each row the same width by adding additional frames to either side of the blocks as needed.

When all the rows are sewn together, the main section of the top will be complete. Press the top carefully and square it up.

Following are exact instructions for the framing of each of the seven blocks in *Our Travels*. The order varies from block to block from the standard of starting at the right side, then moving to the bottom, the left side, then the top. Because I kind of knew the look I was after, I deviated from the standard, beginning with Block 1, to achieve the effect I wanted. Feel free to do the same.

Block 1. Sew a red 2"-wide strip to the left side of the motif; a red 2"-wide strip to the top; a 1½"-wide strip to the right side, and another 1½"-wide green strip to the bottom. Press all seams toward the strips.

Block 1

Block 2. First row: sew a 1¾"-wide red strip to the right side of the motif; sew a 1½"-wide green strip to the bottom; sew another 1½"-wide green strip to the left side; sew a 2"-wide red strip to the top. Second row: sew a 2"-wide purple strip to the left side; sew a 2"-wide burgundy strip to the top; sew a 2½" purple strip across the bottom (not the normal order, but I wanted to separate it from the border, which is the same color); finally, sew a 1¾"-wide burgundy strip to the right side. Press seam allowances to strips.

Block 2

Block 3. The piecing order is a bit different on this block. First round: Sew a 1"-wide red strip to bottom of fabric square or quilt block; sew a 1"-wide red strip to left side; a 1½"-wide green strip to top, and a 1½"-wide green strip to right side. Second round: Sew a 1½"-wide burgundy strip to bottom; sew a 1½"-wide burgundy strip to left side; sew a 2"-wide purple strip to top and a 1¼"-wide purple strip onto right side. Press seam allowances to strips.

Block 3

Block 4. This block is pieced in a different order to provide formal balance of the colors. Sew a 2"-wide red strip to the top of the motif and a 1¾"-wide red strip to the bottom. Sew a 1½"-wide green strip to both sides. Press seam allowances to strips.

Block 4

Block 5. This block is pieced as a mirror image to Block 3. First round: sew a 1"-wide red strip to the bottom of the fabric square or quilt block; sew a 1"-wide red strip to the right side; sew a 1½"-wide green strip to the top, and a 1½"-wide green strip to the left side. Second round: sew a 1½"-wide burgundy strip onto the bottom and a 1½"-wide burgundy strip onto the right side; sew a 2"-wide purple strip to the top and a 1¼"-wide purple strip to the left side. Press all seam allowances to the strips.

Block 5

Block 6

Block 7

Block 6. First round: sew a 1¾"-wide red strip to left side; sew a 2"-wide red strip to top; sew a 1½"-wide green strip to right side and a 1½"-wide green strip to bottom. Second round: sew a 2"-wide purple strip to right side and to bottom; finish with a 3¼"-wide burgundy strip on the left. Press all seam allowances to the strips.

Block 7. First round: sew a 2"-wide burgundy strip to the right side; sew a 1½"-wide green strip to te bottom and the left side; sew a 1¾"-wide burgundy strip to the top. Second round: sew a 2"-wide burgundy strip to the right side. Press seam allowances to the strips.

Square up each block as necessary. (See "Squaring the Quilt Top," page 35.) Make the top row by sewing together Blocks 1 and 2, the middle row by sewing together Blocks 3, 4, and 5, and the bottom row by sewing Blocks 6 and 7 together. Sew the rows to one another in the correct sequence, and square the top once more.

To make the borders, measure through the vertical center of the quilt and trim the strips for the side borders to this measurement. Pin side border strips in place, matching centers and ends. Sew in place; press seam allowances toward borders. Next, measure through the horizontal center of your quilt; trim the strips for the top and bottom borders to equal this length. Pin top and bottom border strips in place, matching centers of borders to center of quilt and ends of strip to outer edges of top; sew in place and press the seam allowances toward borders.

STEP 3. Finishing
Follow the directions for "Squaring the Quilt Top" (page 35), "Assembling the Quilt/Machine Quilting" (page 36), and "Binding the Quilt" (page 38), or, alternatively, "Assembling the Quilt/Tying It" (page 37). Be certain to label your work (page 40).

Our Precious Planet

Made by the author in Fairhaven, Massachusetts in 2003. Quilted by Cathy Franks, Carmel, Indiana. Collection of the author, Indianapolis. Finished size: 41" X 44".

I had my Earth Day tee shirt, a favorite, and I wanted to make a quilt with it that depicts our beautiful planet, our home. It took some time for me to locate other shirts with designs I deemed appropriate. I ended up going to a Salvation Army store in Mattapoisett, Massachusetts, where I located the Ayers Rock and tropical fish shirts. Once I had my shirts, I began looking for support fabrics. Although I love prints, I didn't want my motifs to be lost in a busy background. I prevented that by framing each motif in a dark color, which gave me the opportunity to use Kaye England fabrics that I just loved for the sashing and the borders.

If you compare *Our Precious Planet* with the previous project, *Our Travels*, you will notice that the rows in that quilt were horizontal; in this project, they are vertical. The length of the rows in this project must be the same, although they can be of different widths. In *Our Travels*, it was the opposite: the rows had to be the same width, but the height was not uniform. Both are very flexible quilt plans—between the two of them, you should be able to find an answer to most any design challenge.

Materials

- Five tee shirt motifs, three of which are vertical rectangles, two of which are horizontal rectangles (see "Cutting The Tee Shirts," pages 14-15)
- Specialty fabric to fill in as a motif (I used a border print): strip at least 15" wide by 4" tall
- Framing and second border fabric (black): 1⅓ yards
- Sashing and first border fabric: ½ yard
- Outside (third) border fabric: ⅔ yards
- Backing: 1½ yards
- Batting: 1½ yards
- Binding: ½ yard

Block Layout for "Our Precious Planet"

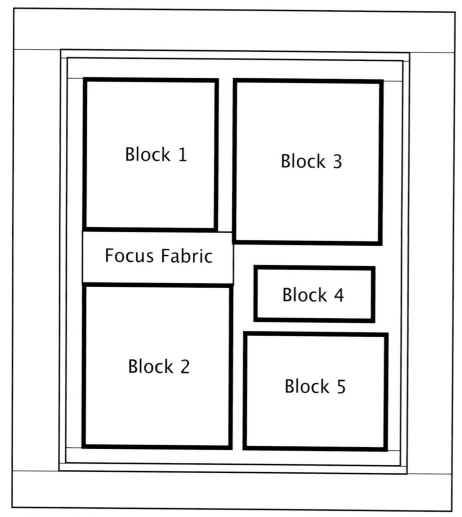

STEP 1. Cutting

Tee shirt motifs: cut one 12" wide by 12½" long (for Block 1); cut two vertical motifs 14" wide by 14½" long (for Blocks 2 and 3); cut one horizontal motif 11" wide by 5" long (for Block 5) and another 12" wide by 10½" long (for Block 6).

Stabilize all the motifs. (See "3. Size the blocks," page 18 and "4. Stabilize the blocks," page 19. Be certain to follow directions for adding seam allowances and for keeping the corners square. You will also need to follow the advice for working with square tee shirt blocks.)

Black framing and (very narrow) second border: cut across the width of the fabric (selvage to selvage) five ¾" wide strips, one 1"-wide strip, and four 1¾"-wide strips.

Sashing and first border: cut across the width of the fabric four 1¾"-wide strips, one 2"-wide strip, one 1¼"-wide strip, one 1½"-wide strip, and one 2¼"-inch wide strip.

Outside (third) border: cut across the width of the fabric four 5½"-wide strips.

Batting and backing: cut to 47" wide by 50" long.

Binding: see Finishing.

STEP 2. Sewing

Frame the motifs: Begin with Block 1. Use the 1"-inch wide black strips, sewing the side frames in place first. Press strips and seams toward strips. Trim the strips even with the top and bottom edges of the motif. Add top and bottom framing strips in the same way.

Frame the remaining blocks in the same manner, using the ¾"-wide black strips on all.

Sash the framed motifs: To **Block 1**, sew a 2"-wide strip of sashing fabric at right-hand side. Press strip and seam toward sashing. Trim ends of sashing even with framing strip.

To **Block 2**, sew a 1¾"-wide strip of sashing across the top. Press strip and seam toward strip. Trim ends of sashing even with framing strip.

Block 3 has no sashing.

Block 4, the smallest block, is sashed as follows: sew a 2¼"-wide sashing strip to the left side of the block and a 1¾"-wide strip to the right side; press strips and seams toward strips and trim edges of strips even with framing. Sew a 1¼"-wide sashing strip across top of block and a 1¾"-wide strip across bottom of block. Press strips and seams toward strip and trim edges even with framing.

Block 5 requires a 1¾"-wide strip on the left side of the block and a 1¼"-wide strip on the right side. Apply as described above.

Square all blocks. (See "Squaring the Quilt Top," page 35.)

Sew right-hand side of quilt together. Sew Block 3 to Block 4. Sew Block 5 to Block 4.

In the left-hand side of the quilt, the focus fabric (a border print in my quilt, but could also be of sashing fabric) is cut to the exact width of Blocks 1 and 2 and to a length (plus seam allowances all around) that will make this vertical row exactly equal to the other. It should be cut to size only at this point, and should measure approximately 14¼"wide by 3½" long. Sew it to the bottom of Block 1, including the sashing at the right of Block 1. Sew Block 2 to the bottom edge of the focus fabric.

Sew the two vertical rows together to make the body of the quilt. Press and square up. (See "Squaring the Quilt Top," page 35.)

For the first border, measure through the vertical center of the quilt. Cut two 1¾"-wide sashing strips to that length. Sew one to each side of the quilt. Press seam toward border. Measure through the horizontal center of the quilt and cut the top and bottom borders from

Top to bottom: Blocks 1, and 2.

Top to bottom: Blocks 3, 4, and 5.

the 1¾"-wide sashing strips to equal that measurement. Sew borders in place and press seams toward borders.

For the second border, use the ¾"-wide black framing strips and follow the steps for the first border—sides first, then top and bottom.

For the third border, use the 5½"-wide strips and follow the same procedure—sides first, then top and bottom borders.

STEP 3. Finishing

Follow the directions for "Squaring the Quilt Top" (page 35), "Assembling the Quilt/Machine Quilting" (page 36), and "Binding the Quilt" (page 38), or, alternatively, "Assembling the Quilt/Tying It" (page 37). Be certain to label your work (page 40).

Adapt the size of the blocks as needed

If the sizes of the blocks given in the preceding directions do not suit your needs, do not let that prevent your using this quilt plan. Simply cut blocks to the size you require, and use sashing in different widths to make everything fit together. You won't need framing if there is enough contrast between the color of the motifs and the sashing fabric. However, this quilt seems to look best if there is an inside border of the sashing fabric, so do not eliminate it. Also, be sure to keep the wide outer border, and make it of a spectacular fabric!

Sawtooth Star

Made by the author in Indianapolis, 2005. Collection of Dr. Jay Schuetz, Decatur, Illinois. Finished size: 38" X 38".

During his senior year of high school, our son was singled out for the honor of representing his class at Boys' State, a week-long event held at Indiana State University. During the week, the boys are given opportunities to learn how state and local governments work by participating in activities such as political races and city planning. This special one-block quilt began with the convocation's gift tee shirt.

Any square motif can become the center of a *Sawtooth Star*. You need to remember only one basic rule: the rectangles that contain the two star points are one-fourth the size of the center motif. For example, if the motif measures 14" wide and 14" deep, the surrounding squares will be 7" wide and 7" deep. It follows, then, that the finished star block will be twice the size of the original motif.

The Boy's State motif began as a 12" square, but with the star sections added, it became a 24" square. I enlarged it further with the addition of a narrow, one-inch-wide inside border that matched the background and "floated" the star inside its three-inch wide border.

Materials

- One tee shirt motif (see "Cutting The Tee Shirts," pages 14-15)
- For background and narrow inside border: ²⁄₃ yard of white or light-colored fabric
- For star points and outer border: 1½ yards of accent fabric
- Backing: 1¼ yards
- Batting: 1¼ yards
- Binding: ⅓ yard

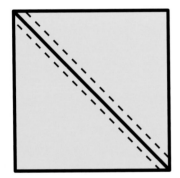

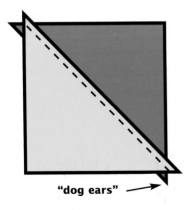

"dog ears" ➔

**Diagram for making half-light,
half-dark squares**

STEP 1. Cutting

Cut tee shirt motif to 12½" square and stabilize it. (See "3. Size the blocks," page 18 and "4. Stabilize the blocks," page 19. Be certain to follow directions for adding seam allowances and for keeping the corners square. You will also need to follow the advice for working with square tee shirt blocks.)

From background fabric, cut four 1½"-wide strips across the width of the fabric. Cut four 6⅞" squares, then cut in half on the diagonal to make eight half-square triangles; cut four 6½" squares.

From accent fabric, cut four 6"-wide strips across the width of the fabric. Cut four 6⅞" squares, then cut in half diagonally to make eight half-square triangles.

Note: Any time I need to cut multiple squares, I first cut a strip of fabric the width I need—say 6⅞"—then cross-cut the strip into 6⅞" squares. If I need squares in two colors, as in this example, I cut strips of the correct width in both colors, place them right sides together, then cross-cut into four squares. The resulting pairs of squares are all ready for marking and sewing.

STEP 2. Sewing

Make four sets of light and dark squares with right sides together. With light square up, draw a diagonal line from corner to corner, then draw two more lines exactly ¼" on either side of the first line. Stitch on the ¼" lines. Cut on the center line. Each set of squares will yield two half-light, half-dark squares, which will become the points of the star. Press seam allowances to the dark half, and trim off the "dog ears" at both ends of seamline. Repeat for all four sets to obtain eight star points.

Lay the triangle squares and the corner blocks around the tee-shirt motif as shown to make a star. For the points on the side of the star, sew two triangle squares together with dark triangles at top and bottom, then sew that unit, with the bases of the dark triangles toward the center, to one side of the tee block. Repeat for the other side of the block. Press seam allowances toward dark triangles.

To make top and bottom rows, first sew two triangle squares together so that dark triangles are on the outside. Add a light corner square to both dark triangles, so that each complete row consists of four squares. Press seam allowances to the dark triangles.

Sew top and bottom rows to the block, with bases of dark triangles toward the center, and press seam allowances toward dark triangles. Then press entire block and measure to make sure it is exactly 24½" square (which will finish to 24"). Square up the block if needed. (See "Squaring the Quilt Top," page 35.)

The first, very narrow, border makes the star seem to "float," because it is of the same fabric as the background. Trim two of the 1½" wide strips of background fabric to the length of the star block and sew one to either side. Press seam allowances to the border.

Measure the width of the block with the side borders in place and cut the two remaining 1½" wide strips to that length. Sew one strip to the top and the other to the bottom. Press seam allowances toward border.

(A note about the narrow inside border: when you make a quilt with numerous stars, it makes sewing the blocks together a great deal easier, because you won't have to match up the star points. This border does not have to match the background in color; contrasting fabric will give you an entirely different look.)

To make the outer borders, first measure through the vertical center of your quilt; trim the strips for the side borders to equal this length. Pin side strips in place, matching centers of borders to center of quilt and ends of strip to outer edges of top; sew in place and press the seam allowances toward borders.

Measure through the horizontal center of the quilt and trim the strips for the top and bottom borders to this measurement. Pin strips in place, matching centers and ends. Sew in place; press seam allowances toward borders.

STEP 3. Finishing

Follow the directions for "Squaring the Quilt Top" (page 35), "Assembling the Quilt/Machine Quilting" (page 36), and "Binding the Quilt" (page 38), or, alternatively, "Assembling the Quilt/Tying It" (page 37). Be certain to label your work (page 40).

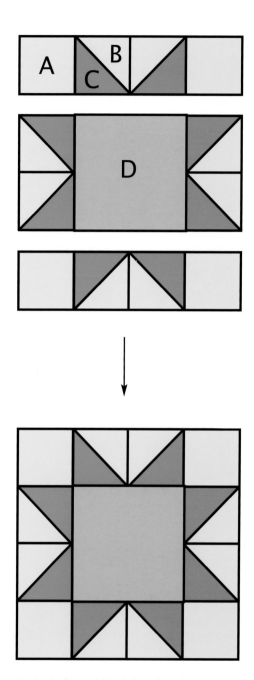

Diagram for making star points

"Stars with a Tee," made by Deborah Oliver in Jefferson City, Tennessee, in 2000. 80" X 80". Collection of the maker.

Sawtooth stars provide a colorful setting for a collection of tee shirt motifs that might otherwise have been difficult to work into a harmonious blend. The tee shirts belonged to Deb's son, Nicholas, when he was about five years old. They lived in Springfield, Illinois at the time, so this quilt sets both a time and a place in memory for the family.

How to Use This Block Design

The star is adaptable to any size motif. All you have to remember is that the finished block will be twice the size of the original motif. The original motif must, however, be a square.

To work out the size of squares that will complete the design (See sizing chart below left) simply divide the length of one side of the motif square in two. In the foregoing example, the motif was 12" square. Therefore, the surrounding squares would each need to be 6" when finished. To allow for seam allowances on the corner blocks, simply add ½" to make a 6½" square. To allow for seam allowances when making the triangle blocks, you must add ⅞" to the light and dark squares that make up each block.

Consider, also, what happens when you use more that one motif in a project. For example, if the motif measures 14", it will double to become a 28" block. If you decide to set four blocks together, two across and two down, the quilt immediately becomes 56" x 56". If you "float" the blocks with a 1"-wide strip of background fabric around each block, the quilt becomes 60" x 60". Add a border, let's say 3" wide, and the quilt becomes 66" x 66".

But, if you add a third row—only two more motifs—to make a six-block set, the measurements become 66" x 96", ideal for twin-size quilt. A full-size quilt can be made with only nine motifs, set together block-to-block, as shown in "Stars with a Tee."

Sizing Chart

Motif size (D)	Corner squares (A)	Triangle Squares (B, C)
10"	5½"	5⅞"
12"	6½"	6⅞"
14"	7½"	7⅞"
16"	8½"	8⅞"